S0-ACG-240

GIVE THEM WINGS AND LET THEM FLY
Surviving the Loss of a Child

Loyal Publishing Inc.
P.O. Box 1892, Sisters, OR 97759
www.loyalpublishing.com

Copyright © 2000 Kymberli Weed Brady
Cover designed by Kymberli Weed Brady
Interior designed by Kirk DouPonce, David Uttley Design

Printed in the United States of America
International Standard Book Number: 1-929125-13-5

Scriptures are taken from the *One Year Bible* (large print edition).
Tyndale House Publishing, Inc., Wheaton, IL. First printing March 1987. Copyright 1985
ISBN 0-8423-2495-X, Kivar. ISBN 0-8423-2481-X, Cloth

Also used, *The Bible, A Multimedia Experience* (for Windows 3.1 & 95) by Soft Key.
Copyright 1996 The Learning Company, Inc. One Athenaeum Street, Cambridge, MA 02142.
HYB3BE-FI ISBN 1-56434-967-5 SCR 3145:4011

Scripture quotation marked (NIV) is taken from the *Holy Bible, New International Version*®.
Copyright © 1973, 1978, 1984 by International Bible Society.
Used by permission of Zondervan Publishing House. All rights reserved.

Scripture quotation marked (NASB) is taken from the *New American Standard Bible* ®,
© Copyright The Lockman Foundation 1960, 1962, 1963, 1968, 1971, 1972, 1973,
1975, 1977, 1995. Used by permission.

ALL RIGHTS RESERVED
No part of this publication may be reproduced, stored in a retrieval system,
or transmitted, in any form or by any other means—electronic, mechanical, photocopying,
recording, or otherwise—without prior written permission of Loyal Publishing, Inc.

00   01   02   03   04   05   06 — 10   9   8   7   6   5   4   3   2   1

KYMBERLI · WEED · BRADY

GIVE THEM *Wings* AND LET THEM *Fly*

Surviving
the Loss
of a Child

LOYAL PUBLISHING
www.loyalpublishing.com

This book is dedicated to my little Angels, this book is your legacy.

*And, to my father, mentor, and friend, Gene Weed, who went
to be with God before this book was finished.*

ACKNOWLEDGEMENTS

To my husband, John, for lending me your heart while mine healed.

To my son, Cole, for filling my otherwise empty arms with hugs and kisses
when I needed them the most. I am truly blessed to have you in my life.

To my father, Gene Weed, thank you for encouraging me
to write and for sharing your talent with me.

To Rev. Larry Keene, for your words of faith that helped me
come to know God in such a wonderful way.

To Chaz Corzine, for your relentless crusade in
making this dream come true.

To Teri, Charlene, Nikki, Tammy, Joe, Toni and those of you who have
lost your babies, may the words on these pages bring you peace.

And to God, this book marks my journey back to you and
my hope that it will help others find their way as well.

FOREWORD

"Kymberli Weed Brady has gifted us with *Give Them Wings and Let Them Fly,* an extraordinarily moving book for those surviving the loss of an unborn child. Powerfully written with simple honesty, profoundly healing with its compassionate message of hope, it breaks through the boundaries of those who have lost an unborn child and embraces all those who have experienced the deep pain associated with losing a loved one with tenderness and understanding. Rooted in faith and love, it truly is a message from above through Ms. Brady's heart and pen.

For those whose souls ache from the pain of loss...for those who have faith and especially those who have not, *Give Them Wings...* is a 'must read' ...a respectful, spiritual 'road side assistance' in the journey back to Him."

—ANN JILLIAN

*W*hile in the throws of grieving my child,

God, in His mercy gave me a vision and let me know

that He would take care of my child.

In this vision I saw my baby as an angel

on its journey into the light.

The result was this poem, and ultimately this book.

This is the symbolism God chose to communicate

His love and compassion for me,

and not a suggestion that babies are actual angels.

*L*ord, today I sent my baby to you.
Plase give her wings and let her fly.
She was so little, I hope they'll fit.
Teach her how they flutter by.
I'll miss her so, though we'd never met
And I'll never know her smile,
But you needed her and now she's yours,
She was only mine a while.
She'll never know pain
And she'll never know fear,
For I know that You will keep her near.
And now...
I close my eyes to say Good-bye
And watch her fly away to you.
Keep her Lord, and love her 'till
I come home and join you too.

I am thinking of you today my friend
and sharing in your pain.
I know it seems as though your life
will never be the same.
I've taken the same journey before.
It's a road I know too well.
But someone it seemed was always there
to catch me when I fell.
There were the times he carried me
when my legs were much too weak,

and the times he held me close to him
when my lips refused to speak.
There were the times he was my eyes
when mine were full of tears,
and all the times he comforted me
and helped me face my fears.
This friend of mine is there for you,
he's been there all along.
Just reach for him and take his hand,
It's where you now belong.

*Y*our feelings...
are messengers
from deep within your heart.
Listen to them.
They are voices calling
from the path of healing.

The only way out of your pain
is to live through it.

$\mathcal{L}$ook to your heart
for the memories
that might have been
and someday will be.

*T*ake a moment.
Lie down.
Know God's angels
are all around.

See them laughing.
Hear them sing.
Oh what joyful
Heavenly beings!

*T*he same everlasting
Father who cares for you
today will take care of
you tomorrow and every day.
Either He will shield
you from suffering or He
will give you unfailing
strength to bear it. Be at
peace then and put aside
all anxious thoughts
and imaginings.

St. Francis De Sales

What we have once
enjoyed and deeply loved
we can never lose.
For all that we love deeply
becomes a part of us.

HELEN KELLER

What soap is for the body,
tears are for the soul.

JEWISH PROVERB

God's Time...

I often wondered
What all the tiny, angelic beings
Do within the endless light of heaven.
Now I know, for six of those jubilant,
Rosy cheeked angels are mine.

Sometimes I envision them in my prayers
Playing hide-and-seek in the clouds.
With wings slightly ruffled
And halos tilted just so,
As only children do.
I imagine them bringing smiles to those
Who, even in Heaven,
Need such simple pleasures.

I see those pure angelic faces
That will never know pain or loneliness.
And, even though my heart longs for them here,
Heaven needs them too.
But God understands my longing,
And sends them to visit me
In a child's laugh or a summer's dream.

TODAY...

I took all of the cards I received
From family and friends
Expressing their sorrow for our loss
And buried them in the middle
Of my flower garden.
I can't think of a more beautiful place
To house the thoughts and prayers
Of such warm and caring people.

Lord, Hold me now,
Please hold me tight.
I need to know
That there's a light.
Tears fill my eyes,
I cannot see.
I need to know
You're here with me.
I feel so empty
And full of shame.
Please tell me
I am not to blame.
Tell me that
This life so short
Was taken for a reason,
And that someday
I will meet my child,
Once I've lived
My final season.

*Y*ou have a broken heart,
Not a broken body.
And as with all of God's wonders,
It will mend
And be whole again.

Gone from our sight,
But never our memories.
Gone from our touch,
But never our hearts.

AUTHOR UNKNOWN

THE VISIT...

Imagine that "perfect" place

In your mind

And bury your baby there.

Visit your angel in your dreams

Or whenever you need a comforting moment.

Help me with the anger.

Help me with the pain.

Help me see the rainbow

That will surely follow the rain...

EMPTY ARMS...

I wanted so badly to see your smile.
To hold your tiny, perfect little hands.
To guide you through your journey
into the loving world
I had prepared for you.
But now, all I have are the memories
that might have been.

Now all that I know is hazy and blurred,
but then I will see everything clearly,
just as clearly as God sees into my heart right now.

1 Corinthians 13:12

*L*ord,
My due date came today.
I thank You for such a beautiful spring day.
For I am able to replace the emptiness
in my heart and in my arms
with the wonderful newness of life
I have found here in my garden.
The fruit trees are full with buds
anxiously awaiting the day that they will unfold
into fragrant blooms of pink and white.
The tulips and daffodils are once again
making their long journey from a deep sleep
into the wonderful warmth of the sun
soon to show their glory
and welcome a new spring.
Life is everywhere here.

And, even though they will die by year's end,
they will all live again.
I am awed by the revelation that
this incredible process
is so often taken for granted.
I realize now that my baby lives through You.
That You have taken this special little soul
under Your wing.
And that we will meet again one day,
when the sun rises
and welcomes the dawn of a new life.
In anticipation of this,
I am filling my empty arms
with the sights and sounds and warmth
of a new day, a new life, a new hope.

One in every four women

has had a miscarriage.

Among them may be a friend,

relative or neighbor—

women you see and talk with every day.

Share your feelings and your pain with them.

There is strength in numbers.

*E*ven though you will never
hold your baby, you did...
in the most special of places,
if only for a short time.

TODAY...

*W*ould have been your birthday
It is cloudy here, how fitting
Today, we would have finally met you
It's a day worth not forgetting
Today, we would have seen your face
Truly an angel from above
Today, we would have held you tight
And surrounded you with love
Today, we would have looked at you
And given you a name
But today will never happen
And no one is to blame.

LETTING GO...

*G*ive your baby the life
they will never know
by planting a fruit tree close by.
Every year,
as the blossoms turn to fruit,
their memory will produce
the sweetest of nature's gifts.

YOU...

*A*re the Mother—
the guardian of
your baby's memory.
Your heart will hold onto
that memory forever
and keep it in a special place
for you to visit.

*E*ven though I didn't carry you
long enough to bury you,
you have a very special
resting place in my heart.
I visit you there often.

*T*ake time to grieve...
It is your friend,
not your enemy.
Journey through
your heart
and learn from it.
It will not be
an easy journey,
but family, friends
and memories will
help light your way.

I will live and honor you.
I will be your eyes
that see a bright red sunset
against a deep blue sky.

I will share my world with you
and show you many things.
Like puppies playing in the grass
and birds that sweetly sing.

I will save my love for you
and keep it in my heart.
For by doing this I know
we will never be apart.

*C*rying is healing!

I will hide beneath
the shadow of your wings
until this storm has passed.

PSALM 57:12

You left without warning
Such a sudden departure.
I barely had time
to relish your existence.
What once was two,
now only one.
Why do I feel so empty?
Family and friends are so close
and my life is otherwise full,
yet I feel so all alone.
You took a piece of my heart
when you left, but...
it belonged to you anyway.

THINK...

*O*f your babies' deaths
as the ultimate gift,
for they will always be with you.
No one will have ever had
such an impact on your life.

In Heaven, their
angels do always
behold the face
of my Father
which is in heaven.

MATTHEW 18:10

$\mathcal{L}$ife is precious...

for there are
no guarantees.

That's Life.

I shall call you
Angel.
You had a beginning
and an end.
Now you have a name.

*A*nd ever has it been
that love knows not its own depth
until the hour of separation.

KAHIL GIBRAN

❦

*G*od will never
give our hearts
more than our souls
can handle.

TALK...

o your pastor or your spiritual mentor
about your loss. This is a huge test of faith
and he will help you find your way through
the tears and back to the path that will
eventually lead you to Heaven,
where your baby waits for you.

*N*ow faith is...
being sure of
what we hope for
and certain of
what we do not see.

HEBREWS 11:1 (NIV)

*I*f I had a seed
for every time
I thought of you,
my garden
would be full.

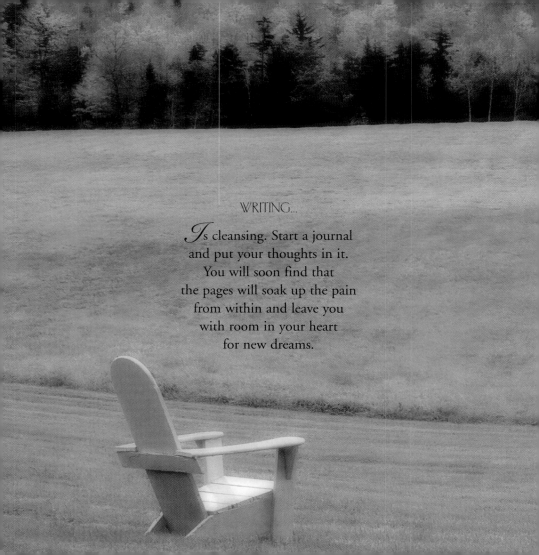

WRITING...

Is cleansing. Start a journal
and put your thoughts in it.
You will soon find that
the pages will soak up the pain
from within and leave you
with room in your heart
for new dreams.

LEAN ON ME...

A friend at this time
can be a most cherished gift.
For not only are they
a memorable part
of your good times,
they can lend a special
comfort to your bad times.
They can offer a tear, a hug,
a sign of love and concern.
All at a time when you
need it the most.

SAVE A PLACE FOR ME.

*Y*ou led the way to heaven today.
Quite a journey, I am sure.
The path you took has lit the way
because your soul was pure.
You took with you my hopes and dreams
for a life you'll never know.
And the loneliness it seems
has filled my heart with woe.

Please un .erstand my little one
I can t see what you see.
One day we'll share forever
for in paradise we'll be.
I'm coming to the place you've found
that you call your very own.
So save a place for me by you
when I make my journey home.

*A*s caterpillars close
their eyes anticipating
the end of their journey,
they awake only to find their
new lives beginning as they
spread their wings to fly.

PRIORITIES...

*C*oncentrate on
mending your body first.
For without proper nutrition
and physical strength,
other losses are sure to follow.
Heal your body,
then your spirit.

WITHOUT YOU MY LITTLE ONE...

Without your smile to greet me
when the day is dawning new,
I wouldn't have the strength I need
to see the hours through.
Without you tugging at my shirt
and wanting me to play,
I don't think I could find the will
to make it through the day.
Without the hugs and kisses
that you so freely give,
I'd never be able to accept
that my babies didn't live.

ANGEL WINGS

A precious angel slipped away,
no one heard a cry.
No time for Daddy and Mommy
to sing me lullabies.
My time with you was much too short,
I had to leave too soon.
But love had joined us as I
grew inside my mommy's womb.
It wove its way within our hearts,
in all our hopes and dreams,
until the very purest love
became my tiny wings.
Although I could not stay with you,
I knew right from the start
that once you felt your angel's love,
you'd keep me in your heart.
I'm just a little angel
but my time was not in vain,
as dark clouds that surrounded you
gave way unto the sun.
My precious parents you will see
that any heart will sing,
if only for a moment
it is brushed by angel wings.

AUTHOR UNKNOWN

Finally the egg and sperm made life
And I begged God to make me more than a wife.
After two long weeks with fingers and toes crossed,
A man came to us in his crisp white coat
And told us, the hopeful parents to be,
That there was to be no hope.
I thought I would cease to exist that day,
The loss in my heart I knew was to stay.
The laughter and promises wrapped up in that egg
Were put to an end confirmed by my blood.
Don't think about the baby I couldn't keep.
The heartache, despair and tears came in floods.
I am sorry to say that I cursed God that day.
And wondered what sin I had committed
To have caused such penance.
And, nobody seemed to care
About the life that I knew was there...
And now, I still wake in the middle of the nigh,t
I'm sweating, the pit in my stomach's so tight.

I'm frightened so deeply, I feel I might scream.
My God tell me they weren't just a dream.
I run to each room to make sure they're still there.
Check each angel face, their breathing, the smell of their hair.
Oh yes they're still here, and I can breathe once again.
And the voice of reason inside my head
Keeps repeating itself to wash out the dread.
It's okay, it's okay, we're a family at last.
I thought the heartache and loneliness would be over.
Thought I was cured when I had my first daughter.
But I was wrong and the seven long years
Of emptiness, pains, failures and fears
Have left scars that are running quite deep.
And I pray they'll become easier to keep.
I try to make use of this, I try to make sense
And remember to thank the Lord for His gifts.
Because whatever this life brings, wherever they go,
I'll never, not ever, have to be told
How precious it is these two lives that I hold.

CHARLENE SARNECKI

There is
a part of me
protecting me,
holding me,
healing me.

*I*n this sad world of ours, sorrow comes to all.
It comes with bitterest agony.
Perfect relief is not possible, except with time.
You cannot now realize that you will ever feel better.
And yet this is a mistake.
You are sure to be happy again.
To know this which is certainly true,
will make you become less miserable now.
I have experienced enough to know what I say.

ABRAHAM LINCOLN
(who lost 3 sons)

GOOD MORNING
LITTLE ONE.

I thought I'd take a moment,
close my eyes, and visit you
in our special place. I wanted
to let you know that I was
thinking about you today...

...and that I love you.

$\mathcal{M}$ay he grant you
your heart's desire
and fulfill
all your plans.

PSALM 20:4

A friend loves
at all times.

PROVERBS 17:17 (NASB)

This is a good time to call on a friend.

MY ANGEL BABY

Once an idea conceived in mind
and then in body.
Nurtured, loved and cared for,
although we never met.
An impression left within my heart
I never will forget.
Why did you exit so quickly?
My opportunity to love someone else.
The lesson is in the seed.
The lesson is in me.

TERI NOEL

A TIME...

*T*here was a time for love,
a time for dreams,
a time for anticipation.

There is a time for loss,
a time for sorrow,
a time for faith.

There will be a time for hope,
a time for joy,
and a time for life.

*There are three things
that remain—
faith, hope and love—
and the greatest of these is love.*

1 Corinthians 13:13

*B*e their eyes...
Get up early and take a walk
in the mornings.
Take your thoughts of them
to your favorite places.

Let them hear
the gentle sounds of nature,
and smell the sweetness
of a new day dawning.

*I will lie down in peace
and sleep,
for though I am alone,
Oh L*ORD*,
you will keep me safe*

PSALM 4:8

*In my distress
I screamed to the LORD
for His help.
And He heard me from Heaven;
my cry reached His ears.*

PSALM 18:6

*A*ngels descending,
Bringing from above,
Echoes of mercy,
Whispers of love.

FANNY J. CROSBY

*T*his was not only
the death of your child,
it was the death
of your dream.
Have faith in new dreams.
For with faith,
all things are possible.

*L*et the little children
come to me,
and don't prevent them.
For of such is the Kingdom
of Heaven.

MATTHEW 19:14

They who sow
in tears
shall reap joy.

PSALM 126:5

WHY...

After having safely
given birth before,
do I not feel
so safe anymore?
Why do I feel like
such a failure,
so incomplete?
Please help me to see this
not just as an ending,
but also a beginning.
Help me to find Your peace.

FAITH...

*I*s so important now.
There is a reason why
some babies have been taken.
Don't waste valuable energy
trying to understand or accept it.
Know that God is taking good care
of your little ones
and will return them to you one day.
Rejoice that they are
in the best of hands
and waiting patiently for you.

There is so much love
when you're
expecting a child.
Love that is
torn from your heart
when your baby dies.
Remember,
there is still room
in your heart
for more dreams,
more love.

I lie awake and look above
into the dark night sky,
and wonder if that was your star
I just saw racing by.
It must be you,
your sparkling soul
shining oh so bright.
It's your gentle way
of telling me
that everything's alright.

*Y*our life was taken
from my world;
but God replaced you
with a rose,
sprinkling petals on
my saddened path
and sunshine
on my woes.

AUTHOR UNKNOWN

*E*ven though I have lost six now, it comforts me to know that they are at least together, that they have each other until I can be with them.

$\mathcal{W}$hat lies behind us
and what lies before us
are tiny matters
compared to what lies
within us.

RALPH WALDO EMERSON

*G*ive me faith.
Give me time
To heal these
Painful wounds
of mine.

AN INVITATION...

*T*o leave a legacy for your baby
by sharing your thoughts
and feelings with others who
desperately need to hear them.

Give Them Wings...II
will be a compilation of writings
from you and others who wish to come together
in the healing process. Send your thoughts to:
email: letthemfly@aol.com
or call: 800.642.9312